S[UMMARY] & ANALYSIS

OF

EVERYTHING IS FIGURE OUTABLE

A GUIDE TO THE BOOK
BY MARIE FORLEO

BY ZIPREADS

NOTE: This book is a summary and analysis and is meant as a companion to, not a replacement for, the original book.

Please follow this link to purchase a copy of the original book: https://amzn.to/2Om6sSz

Copyright © 2019 by ZIP Reads. All rights reserved. This book or parts thereof may not be reproduced in any form, stored in any retrieval system, or transmitted in any form by any means—electronic, mechanical, photocopy, recording, or otherwise—without prior written permission of the publisher, except as provided by United States of America copyright law. This book is intended as a companion to, not a replacement for the original book. ZIP Reads is wholly responsible for this content and is not associated with the original author in any way.

TABLE OF CONTENTS

SYNOPSIS 1

CHAPTER SUMMARIES & KEY TAKEAWAYS 2

CHAPTER ONE: The Tropicana Orange 2

Key Takeaway: Knowing that everything is figureoutable can help you solve a wide range of life challenges. 2

Key Takeaway: Before we think of solving collective problems, we must first change ourselves. 3

CHAPTER TWO: Your Road Map to Results 4

Key Takeaway: There are two major thoughts that will threaten your ability to change your mindset. 4

Key Takeaway: Never accept the belief that some things are too complex to be figured out. 4

Key Takeaway: To reap the results you desire, you must be willing to take action. 5

CHAPTER THREE: The Magic of Belief 5

Key Takeaway: You have the power to create your own reality using your mind. 6

Key Takeaway: Your beliefs have the power to affect your mind, body, spirit, and soul. 6

Key Takeaway: Your beliefs in life are shaped primarily by five factors. 7

CHAPTER FOUR: Eliminate Excuses 8

Key Takeaway: Your bullshit excuses are based on two specific words in your vocabulary. 8

Key Takeaway: To overcome your perceived limitations, you must tackle three core excuses. 9

CHAPTER FIVE: How to Deal With the Fear of Anything 10

Key Takeaway: See fear as a tool rather than an enemy to shrink from. 10

Key Takeaway: Fear is the GPS that guides your soul on where it needs to go. 11

Key Takeaway: To conquer your fears, you must learn to articulate them. 11

Key Takeaway: The way you interpret your emotions will determine your actions. 12

Key Takeaway: See your failure as a learning curve. 13

CHAPTER SIX: Define Your Dream 13

Key Takeaway: Avoid confusion and time-wasting by clarifying your dreams. 13

Key Takeaway: You already have the solution to your problems within you. 14

Key Takeaway: Writing down your goals is almost half the job done. 15

CHAPTER SEVEN: Start Before You're Ready 15

Key Takeaway: Take a trip into the future and ask yourself whether you regret your decision. 16

Key Takeaway: Action generates the courage you need to make progress. 16

Key Takeaway: There are three things to consider on how to start before you are ready. 17

CHAPTER EIGHT: Progress Not Perfection 18

Key Takeaway: Develop a growth mindset over a fixed mindset. 18

Key Takeaway: There are six strategies to use to break free from the bondage of perfectionism. 19

CHAPTER NINE: Refuse to Be Refused 20

Key Takeaway: When things don't go your way, you must be willing to do whatever it takes. 21

Key Takeaway: Be grateful for your haters by transmuting their negative energy into greater motivation. 22

Key Takeaway: Practice three tactics to help you deal with criticism. 22

Key Takeaway: Let your purpose fuel your persistence. ... 23

CHAPTER TEN: The World Needs Your Special Gift 23

Key Takeaway: If you are not chasing your dreams, you are stealing from everyone. 24

Key Takeaway: Don't allow the Imposter Syndrome to prevent you from reaching for your destiny. 24

Key Takeaway: "I wish I had" are the four worst words to ever say. 25

EDITORIAL REVIEW 27
BACKGROUND ON MARIE FORLEO 30

ZIPREADS

SYNOPSIS

Marie Forleo describes how one of her philosophies has changed her life as well as those of countless others. Forleo uses her personal and business experiences to explain how everything in life can be figured out as long as you do not give up.

Forleo starts off by narrating her childhood. Growing up with a single mom in a poor household taught her to always believe that everything is figureoutable, no matter how hard life gets. She proceeds to present a roadmap that anyone can use to figure out their life challenges. She recommends that you avoid making BS excuses and instead take action to solve your problems.

Forleo also talks about the importance of developing empowering beliefs that can help you overcome your fears. Fear is merely a tool that you should use to define your goals clearly and pursue your purpose. Instead of waiting until everything is perfect and in place, just start moving toward your dream. Ultimately, you will figure it out along the way.

Every chapter ends in a testimonial of how different individuals used her philosophy to overcome various challenges. The book also includes exercises in question format to help you integrate what you have learned in each chapter.

CHAPTER SUMMARIES & KEY TAKEAWAYS

CHAPTER ONE: THE TROPICANA ORANGE

Forleo opens the book by explaining how she came up with the concept of "Everything is figureoutable.' She narrates how, during her childhood, her mother received a tiny radio shaped like an orange. At the time, they survived on coupons, and the small orange radio with a straw for an antenna was her mother's most prized possession. Due to their dire financial situation, Forleo's mother would undertake all the repair work in the house herself, including fixing the roof and plumbing work.

When Forleo asked her mother how she knew how to fix all the different stuff around the house, she replied that nothing in life is too difficult to be figured out, as long as you are willing to do the hard work necessary to solve the problem. Therefore, this became Forleo's most powerful mantra in life.

Key Takeaway: Knowing that everything is figureoutable can help you solve a wide range of life challenges.

Forleo says that no matter what kind of negative situation you are facing in your life, knowing that everything can be figured out is the first step to breaking free. She claims that this philosophy helped her end an abusive relationship, win work-study gigs, and even become a professional dancer with no formal training. This philosophy can even be applied when a person in dealing with the loss of a loved one, a negative health diagnosis, or even mental illness.

The reason why most people don't believe this is that the education system doesn't teach students how to tap into their personal power. If people are trained to harness the power of their mind, emotions, and bodies, they will be able to solve all kinds of problems, from the mundane to the complex.

Key Takeaway: Before we think of solving collective problems, we must first change ourselves.

The world today is inundated with all kinds of social, economic, political, and environmental strife. According to Forleo, about 350 million people globally suffer from depression, and the suicide rate in America is at a 30-year high. One billion people are going hungry yet tons of food is thrown out every day. The world is also faced with inequality, racism, violence, and injustice.

But despite our best efforts as a collective, we cannot change the planet unless we first work on ourselves as individuals. Forleo states that through the "everything is figureoutable" philosophy, every individual can transform their own life. It is only then that we can come together to bring about real change globally.

CHAPTER TWO: YOUR ROAD MAP TO RESULTS

In this chapter, Forleo provides a five-step roadmap that can help you achieve the results you need using her philosophy.

Key Takeaway: There are two major thoughts that will threaten your ability to change your mindset.

Whenever you want to embrace a new idea, your brain is likely to rebel against you. The same applies when you decide to learn the "everything is figureoutable" concept. According to Forleo, two major destructive thoughts will hold you back:

- I already know this – To avoid this negative thought, ask yourself what you can learn from the information and how to better execute on it.

- This isn't for me – Instead, ask yourself how this can work for you so that you train your mind to perceive new possibilities.

Key Takeaway: Never accept the belief that some things are too complex to be figured out.

It's easy to make excuses and say that the tools Forleo provides won't work for your particular situation. However, she advises that you at least try out her hypothesis before you give up on it. Even if her philosophy isn't entirely accurate, believing that everything is figureoutable is a very powerful and useful idea. But if you decide that it won't work, then it definitely won't, and nothing is likely to work for you anyway.

Key Takeaway: To reap the results you desire, you must be willing to take action.

There are a lot of books out there that are written to inspire and inform the readers. Forleo claims that her book is meant to take you deeper and farther than that. She states that she wants to help people achieve tangible results. However, this will only be possible if you are totally committed to taking action. This is why she provides Action Challenges at the end of every chapter. By writing down the exercises in a journal and doing the recommended work, you'll be able to change the direction of your life.

CHAPTER THREE: THE MAGIC OF BELIEF

Forleo describes her life journey and career path as a roller coaster that seemed to be leading her nowhere. After graduating from college, she was hired as a trading assistant at the NYSE on Wall Street. Despite the lucrative position, she felt empty and miserable because she believed that her destiny lied elsewhere. She resigned and went on to work as a bartender, ad sales assistant, fashion assistant, life coach, and many others. Every step of the way, she felt like a failure and moved on to find her true calling, once again. Forleo argues that she kept searching and hoping only because deep down she knew that she would somehow be able to figure everything out.

Key Takeaway: You have the power to create your own reality using your mind.

Everything that you see around you right now began as a thought in the mind of an individual. Everything once existed only in someone's imagination. Forleo says that she discovered the truth behind the power of the mind after she ended up in New York. As a child, she once told her parents that she would someday live in the big city. Little did she know that her thoughts would one day manifest into reality.

Forleo believes that we are all born with the power to create our reality by focusing on our ideas. She states that the creation process starts as a thought and becomes a feeling, behavior, and ultimately a result.

Key Takeaway: Your beliefs have the power to affect your mind, body, spirit, and soul.

Forleo claims that if thoughts can become reality, then the beliefs that underlie every thought are the real driving force that controls your life. She defines a belief as anything that you know with absolute confidence and likens beliefs to the hidden templates that you base your life on. Therefore, before you can change your life, you must change your beliefs.

Belief is what makes the placebo effect so effective when it comes to curing disease. Research also shows that belief can improve your cognitive performance and influence your behavior and results. They affect your financial, spiritual, intellectual, emotional, physical, and cultural lifestyle. Your beliefs have such a huge impact on your destiny, and thus if you convince yourself that something is impossible, then for you, it is.

Key Takeaway: Your beliefs in life are shaped primarily by five factors.

Once you begin to question your existing beliefs, you will realize that some of them are positive while others are not worth maintaining. But where did you acquire these beliefs in the first place? Forleo states that there are five things that influence the formation of beliefs:

1. Environment – Ideas you absorb during childhood from the people around you.

2. Direct Experiences – Situations you go through.

3. Evidence – Ideologies you accept from authoritative sources e.g. preachers, media, doctors, and academics.

4. Examples – Role models you know personally, see on TV, or read about in books.

5. Envisioning – Your intuition, inner voice, and dreams.

CHAPTER FOUR: ELIMINATE EXCUSES

There are many excuses you tell yourself that prevent you from achieving your best in life. Though you set out with the right intentions, your mind somehow seems to work against you. Forleo describes excuses as little lies that limit you and what you are supposed to accomplish. In this chapter, she asks readers to look within themselves, call out their own bullshit, and reclaim their power. She asserts that excuses will kill your dreams and keep you trapped in the prison of your own mind.

Key Takeaway: Your bullshit excuses are based on two specific words in your vocabulary.

Forleo believes that your language is the source of your excuses. The two words that hold you back are "can't" and "won't." Every time someone doesn't feel like doing something, they use the word "can't," as if they are not able to. Yet the truth is that "can't" is just a polite way of saying "won't," which means you are simply not willing to do the work. When you say you can't get up early to exercise, you really mean you won't get up early to exercise. Once you accept this brutal honesty about yourself, then you can stop acting like a victim and take back your power.

Though it's true that there are external forces that may affect your life, taking full responsibility for your actions is the best way to regain control and move forward. If something negative happens to you, you should be able to respond in a way that puts you in the driver's seat of your life. Forleo believes that you can only be truly happy once you accept total responsibility for your life.

Key Takeaway: To overcome your perceived limitations, you must tackle three core excuses.

There are many excuses that you make every single day, despite the fact that you are aware of the damage that excuses do. However, Forleo argues that there are three common excuses that you need to resolve:

- I don't have time – How often do you convince yourself that you don't have the time for something? Yet your schedule is a byproduct of choices you made in the past, so if something is important, *choose* to make the time for it. Stop wasting your attention on social media, emails, and TV. Learn to batch cook for yourself and your family to avoid wasting time on daily meal preparation.

- I don't have money – If you believe that your financial situation is holding you back, maybe it's time to ask yourself what you need the money for. If you want to learn a skill or career, there are tons of free courses online. If you want to start a business, you can access free tools online, get a side job, sell some personal stuff, or simply reduce your expenses.

- I don't know how – This is the weakest excuse of all. In this information age, everything you need to learn is right on your smartphone.

CHAPTER FIVE: HOW TO DEAL WITH THE FEAR OF ANYTHING

People tend to be afraid of things they don't understand. But once you get the right knowledge about something, you no longer fear it. Forleo describes how she crashed her scooter because she had forgotten how to ride one. Instead of taking other people's advice and quitting, she chose to learn how to ride it. After receiving detailed instructions, she was able to spend days riding around the coast of Sicily. If she had given up, she would still be afraid of scooters to this day.

Forleo uses this chapter to discuss the kind of fear that keeps you stuck in mediocrity, not the one that saves your life. Some people choose to live afraid because they haven't taken the time to examine their fear. But once you figure out your fear, you can shift your paradigm and find a unique approach to conquering it.

Key Takeaway: See fear as a tool rather than an enemy to shrink from.

The biggest mistake that you can make is to turn your fear into a large monster that is hell-bent on blocking your progress. Forleo argues that fear is actually a good thing—an emotion that is meant to serve you in a positive way once you understand it. Your fear is life's way of getting your attention so that you can be triggered into taking some kind of action. This is why fear never goes away permanently. Every once in a while, you will feel afraid, so it is foolish to put your life on hold until you aren't afraid. Instead, take fear as a sign that there is an action you need to take to quieten that inner voice.

Key Takeaway: Fear is the GPS that guides your soul on where it needs to go.

According to Forleo, fear is often a signpost that shows you which direction to steer your life. One of the most obvious signs of this is when you have a particular idea that refuses to go away. If you are thinking of engaging in some risky or creative endeavor like writing a book or starting a business, and you feel fearful, it is a sign that the idea in your mind is the right step to take. Fear doesn't mean "Stop! Don't go that way!" It should be interpreted as "Yes! Go ahead with the idea! Do it!" In fact, the more visceral the fear in your heart, the more important it is to pursue that particular path.

Key Takeaway: To conquer your fears, you must learn to articulate them.

The first step in conquering your fears is putting them into the right words. Fear becomes debilitating because most people are vague about them, and thus they fail to question or assess the chances of their fear coming to pass. Forleo recommends that you take the following steps:

1. Write down the worst thing that could happen if you proceed with your fear-inducing idea.

2. On a scale of 1 to 10, rate the chances of the worst-case scenario coming to pass. Make sure it's the worst outcome possible.

3. Visualize this negative scenario coming true and jot down a plan of action that will help you recover from it.

4. Now write down the best-case scenarios. Be as specific as possible.

This exercise will help you see that even if your darkest fears come to pass, it won't be the end of the world. You should be able to adjust your plan accordingly and move forward.

Key Takeaway: The way you interpret your emotions will determine your actions.

Quantum physicists say that everything in the Universe is composed of energy—atoms that vibrate at varying frequencies. The only difference between a good and bad emotion is the frequency of vibration. Therefore, Forleo concludes that fear is the same thing as excitement or anticipation, which is why they share the same physiological responses.

So instead of interpreting the tightening of the chest, numb limbs, and accelerated pulse as fear, choose to perceive these vibrations as positive signs. Relabel your emotions using funny names. For example, tell yourself you are feeling "noony" or "shooshie" instead of using the word "fearful."

Key Takeaway: See your failure as a learning curve.

In life, you can never lose. Even if something doesn't work out, consider it to be a learning step. Forleo recommends that you develop the mindset of winning or learning, but never a losing mentality. Think about every past failure and reinterpret them all as part of your learning process. This will empower you to overcome fear.

CHAPTER SIX: DEFINE YOUR DREAM

Forleo describes how she spent years trying to figure out what to do with her life. Everything around her seemed to be crumbling. But when she finally pursued her dream of dance and fitness, she broke down in tears as she realized that she had finally found her niche. Forleo states that people should stop wondering what to do and instead act decisively on their dreams. Stop thinking about your dreams, define them clearly, and then start doing.

Key Takeaway: Avoid confusion and time-wasting by clarifying your dreams.

Forleo says that the first thing she asks her clients to do is tell her what they want to achieve. If someone is unclear about their dreams, then they are more likely to experience disappointment. Yet nobody is ever taught how to clarify their dreams. This is something that you must figure out yourself by looking within. Once you have defined what you want, never give up on it, no matter how long it takes.

Key Takeaway: You already have the solution to your problems within you.

According to Forleo, you have a magical genie inside you that is constantly guiding your actions. This neurological guide springs to action the moment you clarify and become specific about your dreams. This genie is known as the reticular activating system (RAS). At any given moment, your brain is taking in billions of pieces of information. But your brain neither processes nor ignores all this information. Instead, it filters the data and only allows the important stuff in.

Forleo claims that by clearly defining what you want, you are telling your brain what your priorities are. As a result, your RAS filters out everything that doesn't fit your dreams and only processes information that is relevant to that goal. For example, if your dream is to become an entrepreneur, you will suddenly notice all kinds of business information coming your way. Whether it's on TV, the radio, emails, online articles, or just flashes of creative inspiration. You suddenly become more conscious of solutions that can move you toward your dream.

Key Takeaway: Writing down your goals is almost half the job done.

Forleo quotes a study that shows that if you write down your goals, you are 42 percent more likely to achieve them. This may seem like very elementary advice, but the truth is that the majority of people rarely write down their priorities and dreams. It doesn't even matter what the goal is—winning the lottery, healing from surgery, etc. By simply putting your goals down on paper, you have already done almost half the work necessary to achieve it. Once you write it down, make sure you read it often to keep it on top of your mind.

CHAPTER SEVEN: START BEFORE YOU'RE READY

A lot of times we wait until we feel ready before we venture out of our comfort zone. This often leads to many wasted years and future regret. Forleo narrates how she began her dance and fitness coaching career. After barely getting through a few classes, she was offered a teaching position as a dance instructor. A little while after that, she was offered the chance to join MTV as a dance choreographer. In both cases, she felt grossly inadequate and unqualified. Yet she says that choosing to grab those opportunities helped launch her career as a multi-faceted entrepreneur.

Key Takeaway: Take a trip into the future and ask yourself whether you regret your decision.

Forleo says that it is better to go through the pain of doing something and failing at it rather than living in regret for not making a certain decision. This is the conundrum she faced when she was contemplating whether to pursue dance and fitness as a serious career. After failing in four separate careers, she asked herself whether in 10 years she would regret NOT choosing dance as a career move. Her answer was an equivocal Yes.

Most people engage in "future tripping," where they worry about the future instead of living in the present moment. But you can actually use the same process in a strategic way as a powerful catalyst to move you forward. Look 10 years into the future and see whether you will regret not making the decision that you are currently worried about.

Key Takeaway: Action generates the courage you need to make progress.

When Forleo was offered the chance to become a producer/choreographer with MTV, a little voice in her head told her that she was not ready for such a big move. But she managed to muster up the courage to go to the MTV offices and book the gig. This one opportunity opened up a myriad of doors for her to develop new skills, despite the fact that she was less knowledgeable or experienced than most of her dance students.

Forleo believes that you will only progress in life by making brave decisions that go against your uncertainty and fear. Most people wait to muster courage before taking action, but the reality is that your action must come before your courage. You have to ignore that lazy, whiny voice inside you that says you aren't ready yet.

Key Takeaway: There are three things to consider on how to start before you are ready.

Forleo suggests that you take into account the following three factors to master the art of taking action before you are ready:

Avoid the tendency to waste time in "research and planning" – Most people use this as an excuse not to take advantage of an opportunity when it presents itself. Forleo argues that this is simply a subtle form of procrastination. Don't spend months going down online rabbit holes researching and planning on how to do something. Just start immediately and get the information you need as things become much clearer.

Make a firm commitment – Putting skin in the game is the best way to stay accountable to your goals. Make some kind of financial commitment or get an accountability partner to ensure that there are painful consequences if you fail to follow through.

Prioritize growth and learning – Most entrepreneurs find a comfort zone they would rather stay in instead of doing something risky that will grow their business. Forleo suggests that you get out of your comfort zone and step into the growth zone. For example, if you're running a hectic startup, hire someone to help you. Doing something you've never done before, i.e. delegating some tasks, is how you learn new skills.

CHAPTER EIGHT: PROGRESS NOT PERFECTION

In this chapter, Forleo talks about how perfectionism can stifle your progress and keep you stuck in a negative place for the rest of your life. She admits that she has high personal and professional standards. However, this is very different from perfectionism. While the former is healthy and constructive, the latter is dysfunctional and based on fear. A perfectionist is someone who thinks they are not good enough, and Forleo describes the dangers associated with this kind of thinking.

Key Takeaway: Develop a growth mindset over a fixed mindset.

A fixed mindset is where you believe that talent is all you need to succeed. You don't put in much effort, avoid challenges, hate criticism, and do things just to get approval from others. This kind of attitude is destructive and ultimately blocks your progress.

On the other hand, you can develop a growth mindset. This is where you believe that your basic talents and abilities can get better if you apply a more disciplined effort. Even if you aren't very gifted at something, you know that every challenge is a learning opportunity. As a result, you get better gradually over time. Forleo says that a growth mindset helps you learn, become resilient, and accomplish your goals.

Key Takeaway: There are six strategies to use to break free from the bondage of perfectionism.

Forleo recommends the following six tactics to keep you in the progress rather than perfection zone:

Do the work and ignore the drama – If you want to move toward a goal, avoid engaging in the kind of drama that comes with perfectionism. For example, if you want to start a business, don't worry about whether your idea is good enough, what your family will think, or how everyone will be jealous of you. Just focus on the small steps necessary to get you where you need to go.

Anticipate and solve problems in advance – There is always something that will go wrong, regardless of how organized you are. The secret to progress is to plan ahead. What could potentially interfere with your workday? What could ruin the project? Anticipate these problems and brainstorm ways of handling them.

Expect some self-doubt – Once the euphoria of chasing your amazing dream wears off, self-doubt will creep in. You will question why you decided to follow that path. This is quite common, so don't take it as a sign to quit. Just relax and focus on the next step in your project.

Focus on the next right step – Setbacks are common, and when faced with one, you should ask "What is the best move to take right now?" Listen to your inner wisdom. Maybe you simply need to relax and meditate. Maybe you should consider using that negative feedback from a client to gain better insight.

Positive quitting – Never stick with a project that you know isn't right for you. If something isn't working despite all your best efforts, or if you have lost the passion, just quit and move on. Find something that you truly want and work on that instead.

Patience is a virtue – There are many examples of people who worked for years on projects without reaping any reward from them. Yet they stuck to their creative pursuits and ended up achieving fame decades later. Sometimes you have to be patient and wait for your opportunity.

CHAPTER NINE: REFUSE TO BE REFUSED

Forleo describes how she and her fiancée did everything they could to save their relationship. Even when a flight attendant told them they couldn't board their plane to Barcelona because they were checking in late, Forleo refused to give up. Through sheer will and luck, they made it. She states that sometimes in life, you have to stand your ground and refuse to accept the hand you are dealt. You should always try to question everything you are told so that you develop your strengths and capabilities. By repeatedly refusing to take no for an answer, you can make positive and lasting changes in your life.

Key Takeaway: When things don't go your way, you must be willing to do whatever it takes.

Forleo explains how a group of Liberian women managed to bring their country's civil war to an end through sheer persistence and utilizing the tools they had. When the civil war broke out in 1972, Leymah Gbowee was forced to quit school and flee to a refugee camp. She went on to endure domestic abuse for years and ended up becoming a trauma counselor for the child soldiers of Liberia. In 1999, when the war broke out again, she and her fellow women organized mass sit-ins in open fields, enduring the searing sun and drenching rain every single day for months.

The women even held a sex strike to force the men to stop fighting. When negotiations stalled, they traveled to the hotel where the peace talks were being held and refused to let the delegates leave until they signed a peace agreement. Within a matter of weeks, the war ended and Leymah received the Nobel Peace Prize in 2011. She and her fellow women showed great bravery, resilience, and creativity to figure out what seemed to others like an impossible situation. Forleo says that when you refuse to give up and commit to figuring out your problems, miracles can occur.

Key Takeaway: Be grateful for your haters by transmuting their negative energy into greater motivation.

When you have a dream or goal, there are always people who will make you feel as if your ambitions are useless and irrational. Such criticism can come from loved ones and strangers alike. But this is to be expected for anyone who is trailblazing or making radical changes to their life or business. Forleo states that this criticism is normal and you should use the put-downs as fuel for your ambitions. She explains how a stinging criticism from one naysayer motivated her to make her B-School an even greater success. She recommends that you become an alchemist who can take negative energy and transmute it into productivity.

Key Takeaway: Practice three tactics to help you deal with criticism.

1. Examine the source of the criticism – The majority of successful people rarely have time to harshly judge others because they are busy doing their own thing. Most of your harshest haters will be insecure cowards who haven't accomplished anything. Unless someone has a body of work that you can admire, don't take their criticism to heart.

2. Empathize with your naysayers – People who are hurting are the ones who tend to be the meanest. They are seeking attention and have nothing going for them

so they attack others. Instead of getting angry at your naysayers, feel sad for them.

3. Learn to laugh at unnecessary criticism – When people on social media were making fun of her hair as being fake, Forleo joined in by cracking jokes about herself. This is a way to turn the spotlight on and neutralize petty trolls.

Key Takeaway: Let your purpose fuel your persistence.

According to Forleo, the secret behind a life of persistence is having a greater purpose beyond yourself. Leymah never set out to win the Nobel Prize. All she cared about was creating a peaceful nation where everyone could live a better life. Similarly, Forleo didn't intend to become successful and famous through her work. All she wanted was to serve her team and audience. By having a greater good that goes beyond your own personal interests, you will be able to become unstoppable.

CHAPTER TEN: THE WORLD NEEDS YOUR SPECIAL GIFT

Forleo believes that one of the things that will prevent you from realizing your dream is assuming that your talent is not special or valuable enough to share with others. She reiterates that you have something to offer the world, and there is always at least one person who is waiting to hear your unique voice and perspective.

Key Takeaway: If you are not chasing your dreams, you are stealing from everyone.

Life doesn't make mistakes. If you are here right now, it is for a reason, and you must find that reason and achieve your purpose. Forleo claims that anyone who isn't using their innate powers, strengths, and talents to create change in their life and their environment is a thief. Why? Because they are stealing from those people who need your talents the most!

Only you have your special gift, which means that you are obligated to do something with it to benefit the world. It could be a book, song, movie, business, app, or anything! If you do not manifest what you are supposed to bring forth in this world, you are essentially robbing this and every other generation to come. It doesn't have to be something on a grand scale. Just share whatever abilities you are blessed with to make the world a better place.

Key Takeaway: Don't allow the Imposter Syndrome to prevent you from reaching for your destiny.

There are many famous personalities who, despite their great accomplishments, felt like frauds. Maya Angelou, Jennifer Lopez, and Jodie Foster have all said that at some point in their careers, they felt like imposters, hoodwinking their audience. Therefore, you do not have to feel bad for perceiving your accomplishment to be a mistake. Everybody goes through this, especially women. According to Forleo, there are steps you can take to avoid the imposter syndrome from ruining your destiny:

- Talk about how you feel with others. Share your shame with people who will encourage and remind you of your greatness.

- Create a file filled with compliments, accolades, and positive comments others have made about you. When you feel like a fraud, read the file.

- Shine your light on others instead of fixating your attention on yourself. Compliment and thank others whenever you feel like a fraud.

Key Takeaway: "I wish I had" are the four worst words to ever say.

Forleo quotes the research that a former palliative nurse conducted on her patients. The nurse discovered that the biggest regret of her dying patients was that they never had the courage to live their lives the way they wanted to. Most people are too preoccupied with the opinion of others that they sacrifice their own happiness. At the end of the day, all they are left with are regrets.

How long will you keep saying the words "I wish I had…?" These are the worst four words because they indicate that you failed to muster the courage to live your best life when the opportunity came. You already have all the power and solutions within you, so start believing that everything can be figured out. The world needs you.

EDITORIAL REVIEW

Marie Forleo does it again in her latest book, *Everything is Figureoutable*. In her characteristic in-your-face, no BS New Jersey style, she shows us the power of belief and how it can change your circumstances.

So what does it mean when we say Everything is Figureoutable? It simply means that no matter what kind of situation you are facing, you already have all the answers within you. Only your limiting beliefs, excuses, and fears may be holding you back.

Forleo uses her personal stories to show us the genesis of this life philosophy. When her parents divorced, her mom raised her in dire financial conditions. Her mom had to do all the plumbing, roofing, and electrical work herself because they couldn't afford to pay a professional. Despite not having any technical expertise in these areas, her mom always managed to figure stuff out and fix whatever was needed. When Forleo asked her how she knew so much, her reply was "Everything is figureoutable." This would become the creed that would catapult Forleo to massive success.

In the book, she says that you should never believe that anything is too complex to figure out. Just be prepared to take the necessary action to reap the results you desire. You also need to change your mindset and stop making excuses. Most people assume that they already know everything or worse still, that they are not good enough. It is these limiting beliefs that Forleo seeks to banish from your mindset.

Another concept in the book is that if you are not living your best life, you are robbing the world. There are people who are waiting to be inspired by your gifts and talents. Don't let your small-minded thinking prevent you from having an impact. Sometimes you have to refuse to take no for an answer and stand your ground. Fight for your destiny and focus on progress rather than perfection. Waiting for everything to be perfect will only stall your progress.

Anyone who has watched MarieTV knows what kind of character Forleo is. She offers tough love that will light a fire under your backside. She gladly curses to get her point across, and though her book is laced with some profanity, it's not a turn-off.

The book is filled with witty remarks and funny stories that will lighten your spirits. Forleo really knows her to deliver her punchlines when you least expect it. It is guaranteed that you will learn a lot from her experiences as well as the inspirational stories in each chapter.

At the end of every chapter, she provides a testimonial from an individual who has used her philosophy to transform their life. These stories range from starting a business, overcoming a disease, escaping from abusive relationships, and even raising kids.

This is not a complex spiritual book. Forleo is a very practical gal, and she has made sure that her book is ridiculously simple to read and apply. If you are searching for a simple book that tells it as it is with absolutely no BS, then Marie

Forleo has already figured it out for you. This is the book you need.

BACKGROUND ON MARIE FORLEO

Marie Forleo is an American "multi-passionate" entrepreneur, author, philanthropist, and host of her award-winning show, *MarieTV*. She hosts The Marie Forleo podcast and has created several online training courses. Her first book, *Make Every Man Want You*, was published in 2008 and went on to be translated into 16 languages.

She was born in New Jersey on December 7, 1975. Forleo attended Seton Hall University where she graduated with a Business Finance degree in 1997.

After college, she worked as a trading assistant on the New York Stock Exchange. She then went to work for various fashion and gourmet magazines before starting her journey as a life coach. She has also worked as a bartender, waitress, and fitness and dance instructor. In 2005, Forleo was chosen as one of the initial Nike Elite Dance Athletes.

Forleo founded Marie Forleo International in 2009. The coaching company runs B-School, which is a renowned training program for upcoming entrepreneurs from all walks of life.

She has been named by Oprah as one of the foremost thought-leaders of her generation. Her website MarieForleo.com was named by Forbes as one of the top 100 websites for entrepreneurs.

She lives with her partner Josh in New York City.

END OF BOOK SUMMARY

*If you enjoyed this **ZIP Reads** publication, we encourage you to purchase a copy of <u>the original book.</u>*

We'd also love an honest review on Amazon.com!

Want **FREE** book summaries delivered weekly? Sign up for our email list and get notified of all our new releases, free promos, and $0.99 deals!

No spam, just books.

Sign up at **<u>www.zipreads.co</u>**

Made in United States
Troutdale, OR
09/28/2023

13258537R00022